PARIS

NIGHT & DAY

COLORING BOOK

First edition for North America published in 2016 by Barron's Educational Series, Inc.

© Copyright 2016 by Carlton Publishing Group

All inquiries should be addressed to:

Barron's Educational Series, Inc.
250 Wireless Boulevard
Hauppauge, New York 11788
www.barronseduc.com

ISBN: 978-1-4380-0941-4

Manufactured by: Leo Paper Products Ltd., Heshan, China

Printed in China

9 8 7 6 5 4 3 2 1

For best results, colored pencils are recommended.

PARIS

NIGHT & DAY

COLORING BOOK

ILLUSTRATED BY PATRICIA MOFFETT

CONTENTS

 **ARC DE TRIOMPHE**

 **PALAIS GARNIER**

 **CHÂTEAU DE VERSAILLES**

 **TOUR EIFFEL**

 **SACRÉ-COEUR**

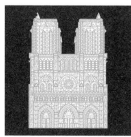 **NOTRE-DAME**

 **PLACE DE LA CONCORDE**

 **PARC DES BUTTES-CHAUMONT**

 **MÉTROPOLITAIN**

MUSÉE BOURDELLE

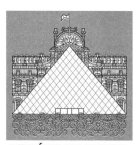 **MUSÉE DU LOUVRE**

 **VERSAILLES COUR DE MARBRE**

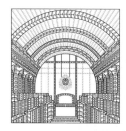 **MUSÉE D'ORSAY**

 **PLACE DE LA BASTILLE**

 **HÔTEL DES INVALIDES**

 **MOULIN ROUGE**

 **PANTHÉON**

 **CENTRE POMPIDOU**

 **JARDIN DES TUILERIES**

 **PONT NEUF**

**JARDIN
DES PLANTES**

PALAIS-ROYAL

**PONT
ALEXANDRE III**

SAINTE-CHAPELLE

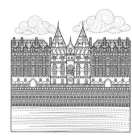

CONCIERGERIE

PLACE VENDÔME

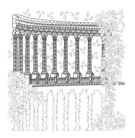

PARC MONCEAU

GRAND PALAIS

**DÔME DES
INVALIDES**

**CIMETIÈRE DU
PÈRE-LACHAISE**

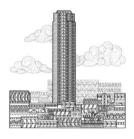

**TOUR
MONTPARNASSE**

MUSÉE RODIN

**PARC DU CHAMP
DE MARS**

ÎLE DE LA CITÉ

PETIT PALAIS

**GALERIES
LAFAYETTE**

MUSÉE DE CLUNY

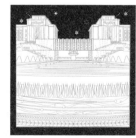

**PALAIS DE
CHAILLOT**

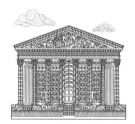

**ÉGLISE DE LA
MADELEINE**

PLACE DES VOSGES

**PARC DE LA
VILLETTE**

PARIS-PLAGES

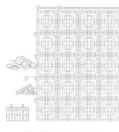

**INSTITUT DU
MONDE ARABE**

QUARTIER LATIN

**JARDIN DES
SERRES D'AUTEUIL**

Introduction

Welcome to a new coloring challenge!

The *Paris Night & Day Coloring Book* is unique because it invites you to color not just against white, but also blue, black, and gold backgrounds. Each of the 90 detailed outlines featured here are displayed against both a day and a night backdrop, providing you with superb opportunities to highlight tone and texture, and create striking contrasts.

While daylight can illuminate subtle motifs and tints, darkness can bring out flashes of color or the sparkle of lights. In fact, you'll find there's a surprising difference between an enchanting Parisian scene depicted in golden sunshine and that same scene shown against a background of inky darkness.

The captivating sights presented in this book range from impressive buildings to beautiful statues, and from pretty parks to magnificent bridges. They include many favorites, such as the Musée du Louvre, Tour Eiffel, Sacré-Coeur, and Notre-Dame, as well as less familiar sights, like the Petit Palais, Institut du Monde Arabe, Tour Montparnasse, Cimetière du Père-Lachaise, and Conciergerie. There is the legendary entertainment venue, the Moulin Rouge, and wonderful outdoor spaces, such as the Parc des Buttes-Chaumont, Jardin des Tuileries, and Parc Monceau.

What was beautiful in the daytime can seem just as stunning at night, and what was subtle in the light can emerge from darkness as striking when night falls. How will your daylight Quartier Latin differ from your midnight version? Could your daytime Château de Versailles sparkle in the moonlight? Might the Musée Rodin come alive after dark?

How you decide to bring out the appearance of a Parisian scene is determined by you and the color choices you make on each artwork. You can be as accurate and realistic, or as creative and fantasy-filled, as you like. Working with the colored backgrounds opens up exciting possibilities and an invigorating new world of coloring, so let your imagination—and your pens—run wild.

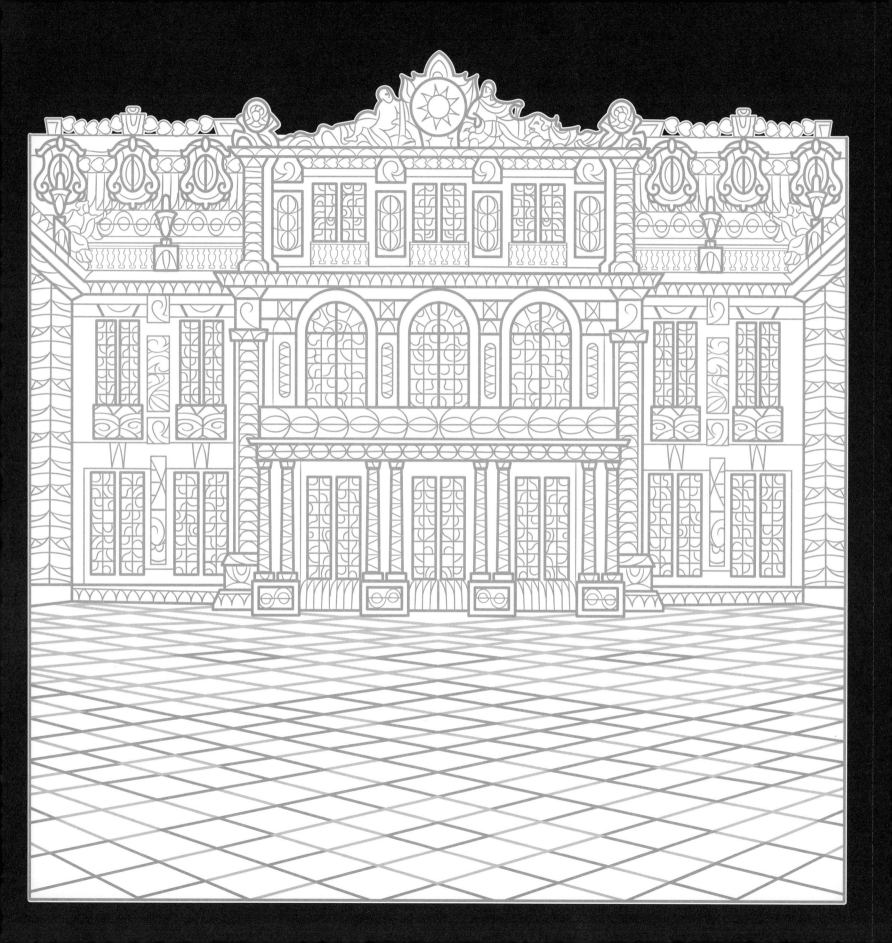

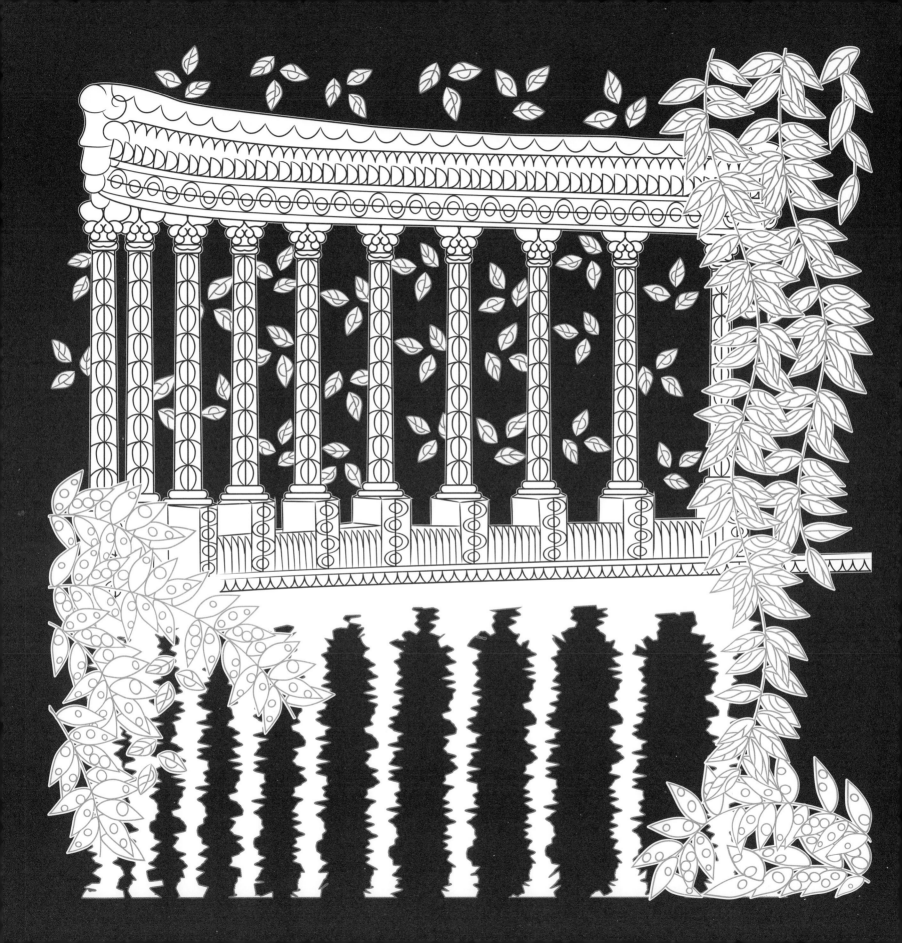

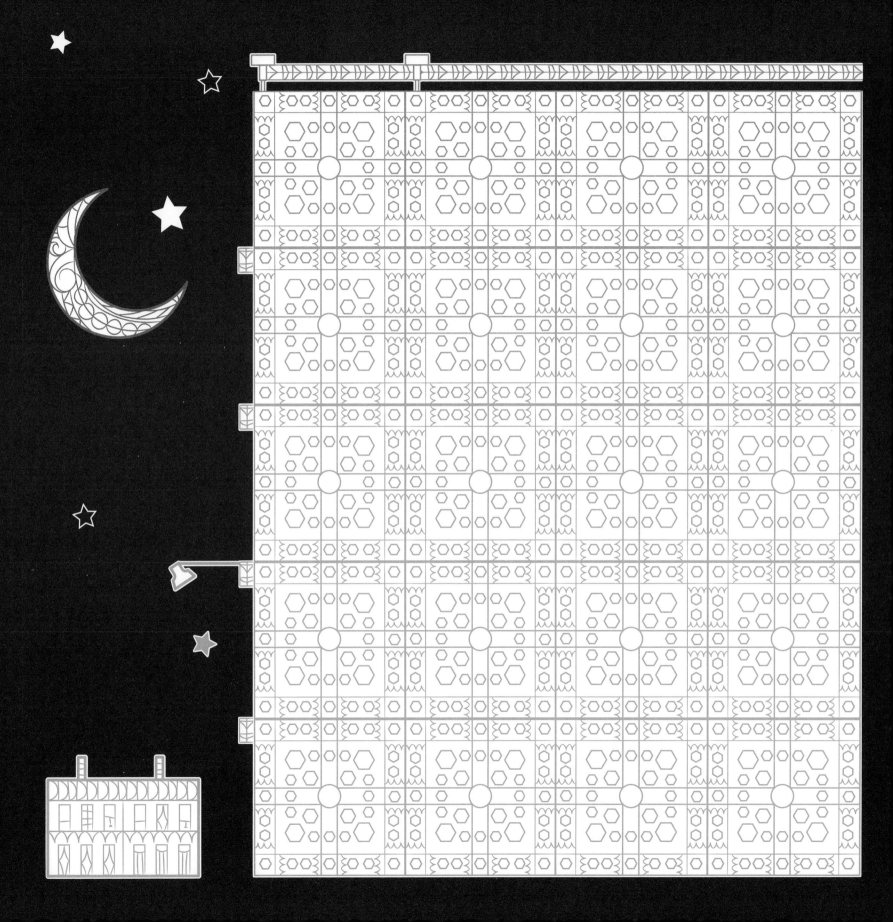

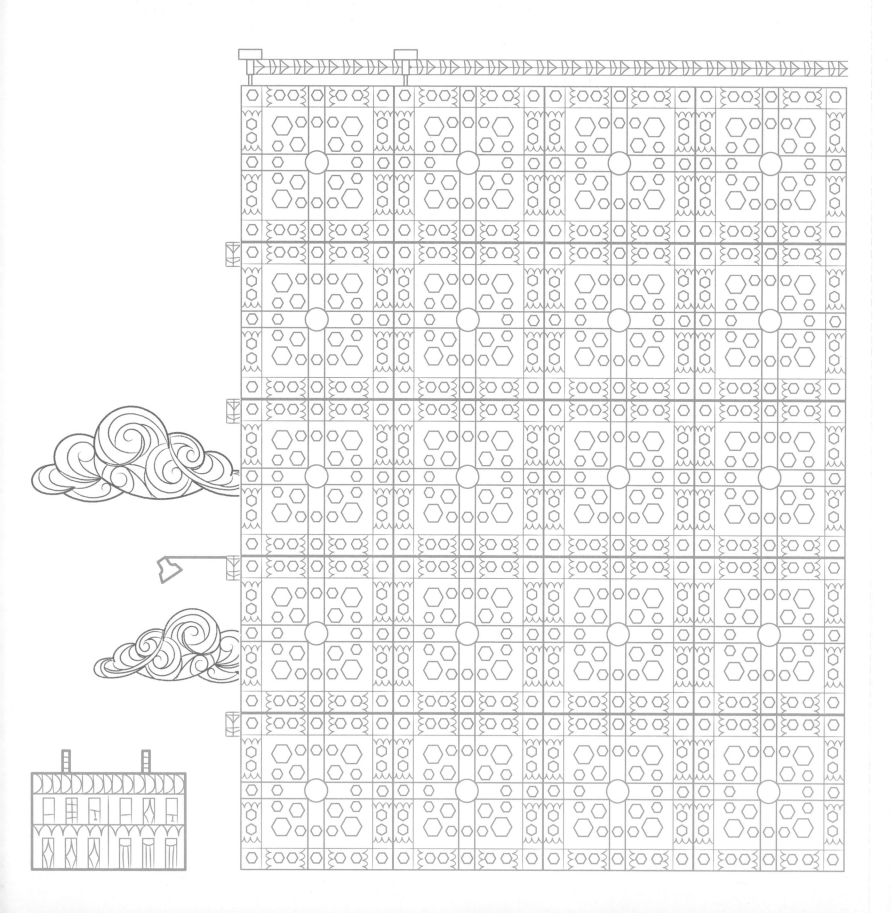